Styled By Independence

A Woman's Journey to
Self-Discovery Through
Adversity

By Brenda Gonzalez

Copyright © 2023 by Brenda Gonzalez

ISBN: 9798866790760

Stronger Through Faith Publishing

www.strongerthroughfaith.com

All rights reserved. No part of this book may be reproduced or transmitted in any form or by any means without the written permission of the author.

TABLE OF CONTENTS

06
CHAPTER 1
Uniform Girl

10
CHAPTER 2
Stitching a Young Girl's Dream to a Young Woman's Reality

13
CHAPTER 3
A Dream Deferred

17
CHAPTER 4
A Wedding, A Baby, and Postpartum Depression

23
CHAPTER 5
Work to the Rescue! ... or Maybe Not

27
CHAPTER 6
The Unstoppable Woman

TABLE OF CONTENTS

31
CHAPTER 7
Building Back Momentum

35
CHAPTER 8
Plan B for The Win!

38
CHAPTER 9
Redesigning Me

41
Connect with Brenda

DEDICATION

This book is dedicated to my Grandma Sybil. She was always a fashion connoisseur. She came to this country from Jamaica and sought a better life for her family and her offspring. She wanted us all to get a good education and to have a piece of the American dream. She wanted us to be happy and do whatever we wanted to do. Grandma Sybil, you would be proud to see what I've done. I want to dedicate this book to my Grandma JJ who came to this country from Panama. She hoped that the generations after her would have a better life through education and faith in God. Grandma JJ, I'm making my "good better, and my better, best..." and I am teaching my children the same.

This book is also dedicated to my two boys who always keep me going and give me a reason to strive to be the best me that I can be.

Chapter 1

UNIFORM GIRL

I stared into my closet wondering what kind of statement I'd make in school tomorrow. I wanted to be noticed like the "uniform girl". "Uniform girl" was a girl in my school who wasn't particularly charismatic or popular but she was the only girl who always had on the uniform in Public School (P.S.) 16 in the Bronx, where I grew up. While uniforms were allowed, they were not mandatory and most of the students did not wear them. Every time "uniform girl" walked into the room or when I saw her run across the schoolyard, she was noticeable. Even if you didn't know her name, you noticed her presence. I wanted to be the best-dressed student at P.S. 16. I wanted the attention that "uniform girl" got all to myself. I looked at my uniform hanging in the closet and I started conceptualizing how I was going to wear it. At the time, I didn't know this was called "styling" the outfit, I just thought, I wanted to fix it up a little bit. It was a one-piece uniform with the X over the top that connected to a plaid pleated skirt. The entire uniform was plaid. It was a dark green and navy blue color. I thought about wearing a shirt over the top of the plaid one-piece uniform so that the bottom would just be a skirt. I thought about wearing a shirt underneath the top X - like "uniform girl". I thought about wearing my favorite headband to coordinate. What shoes would I wear? "Uniform girl" was not going to outdo me tomorrow. In the end, I ended up wearing the clothes my mother told me to wear. It didn't make sense to her why I'd want to wear a uniform after it's been hanging in my closet for almost the entire school year at this point. I understood, but I still wanted to outdo "uniform girl". I never told her this, because surely she would say the idea of suddenly wearing a uniform to school was ludicrous; especially at 6 years old.

To this day, I don't know if I ever outdid "uniform girl". But looking back, my pursuit to stand out has never stopped. A few years later, my family and I moved from the Bronx to Long Island, a suburb of New York City. It was at this point that I noticed life was different on the other side. I noticed that all of the kids had name-brand clothes, the newest toys, and just about everything

they could have wanted. This was the only time that I noticed what I didn't have. Although I didn't stand out as much as "uniform girl" at my old school in the Bronx, I did have a presence of my own. Despite the move to a new location, I still had my friends in the Bronx. It was during this time that I noticed, that to make friends, I'd have to look like the other kids whom I referred to as "the rich kids". I wanted to have the name-brand sneakers and the name-brand logos but being new to the neighborhood, my family couldn't quite afford all of those things. We could afford to live there though. We lived in a big house with a backyard that was all our own. We didn't even have to share it with another family.

This was something I'd never experienced up until this point. I guess making the move had its benefits, it was worth it to live in a big house in a deserted neighborhood. There was never anyone outside. I didn't see any boys hanging out on the street corner like in my old neighborhood. There was no one playing in the open fire hydrants in the summertime, like in the Bronx. I don't even remember if I saw any fire hydrants on my new block. It was a very quiet neighborhood. I hardly saw anyone that looked like me. It was a lonely kind of place but somehow it was better than where we were. Because my family did not have a lot of money for name-brand clothes, I learned to stretch the budget of what I was given to shop for new clothes. I learned to mix and match my items in different ways so that I felt like I was wearing new clothes each time.

I learned to style, without even knowing that I was styling. I learned to take $50 and buy numerous items. My sister, on the one hand, would buy two or three things that she really liked. I, on the other hand, was a clearance rack connoisseur. I was a bargain finder. I was someone who would buy the things that were on sale that no one else wanted and turn them into a fashion masterpiece, you would never even know it came off the clearance rack. I learned to be creative in putting things together because it saved me money. Where I lacked money, I made up for it with creativity. I felt like I had tapped into the term, "One man's trash is another man's treasure". I found so much treasure in the things that no one wanted. It was like a gold mine to see things in my size that I could manipulate into an outfit that was dreamy. As time went by, fashion design was all I thought about. I'd draw sketches in class and daydream about what life would be like as a rich and famous person. My teacher would have to tell me to stay on track with the class lesson. I'd be daydreaming about the music videos I had seen on TV, what the singers would be wearing, how they would dance, and how cool they were. They never seemed to have to go to school and I wish that could be my life. I had big dreams that involved living a high life. I knew I was destined to wear big sunglasses, ride in limos, hang out with celebrities, and attend fancy award shows and red carpet events. I'd live a life where I'd be dodging the paparazzi who would try to take photos of me and I'd say, "No pictures, please". As I got older, I realized that life was more trapping than freeing. The celebrities I had the pleasure of watching through VH1's "Behind The Music" disclosed the woes of fame and I believed it.

Chapter 2

STITCHING A YOUNG GIRL'S DREAM TO A YOUNG WOMAN'S REALITY

When I was about 11, my mother could see how passionate I was about art. She enrolled me in a sketching class at the local recreation center to develop my skills. I learned how to sketch faces and although I missed a lot of lessons, there are some things I still remember.

I had a passion for Fashion Design. I read magazines and conceptualized how I wanted to make something that was different than anything I'd ever seen. I learned that these styles of fashion were called *avant-garde*, *couture*, and *haute couture*. As time went on, my mother bought me a sewing machine. I wasn't really sure how to use it, but I was determined to figure it out. The problem was, I was too excited to sit and read the instructions and threw them away. This proved to be a pivotal mistake. I struggled to figure out how to use the machine for weeks. I finally confessed to my mother one day that I could not figure out how to use it and I thought it was broken. She told me she would get me another one. Time passed and I didn't end up getting a replacement.

What I did find out, years later, is that the foot pedal was disconnected from the machine. This is why it didn't work. It was a simple fix that had I known better, would've been resolved in seconds. Years later in high school, I took Home Economics and learned the basics of how to sew - by hand and with a sewing machine. I learned how a bobbin works, how to thread a needle, how to unclog snags, fabrics, and other basic information. If I had the resources of the children today, like access to YouTube, and social media, I could've been a child prodigy fashion designer. Now, we'll never know.

I loved art and knew I'd be a Creative professional of some sort. At no point did my mother ever tell me I couldn't do it nor did she ever tell me I needed to pick a stable, lucrative job instead. This is unlike what she told me her father said to her when she wanted to be a Flight Attendant.

My mother told me a story where she presented her dream of being a Flight Attendant to my grandfather when she was a teenager in the 70's. He crushed her dream by saying: Flight Attendants were nothing more than "sky waitresses". While that wasn't 100% false, I could see how that would crush her dream of getting a job that she felt was prestigious at the time. Maybe it would have changed the course of her life. Maybe she would have gotten to see the world on the dime of the airline. Now, we'll never know.

My mother made me believe l that I could be whatever I wanted to be. It was a little delusional sometimes, but no matter what I said, she told me I could do it. I even said I wanted to be the President of the United States at one point. This was back in the '90s when there were no black presidents and there were hardly any black people or women in politics. Still, she never made me feel like there was a thing that I couldn't do. I've heard stories from children whose parents steered them into professions, like doctors and lawyers, for the prestige and the salaries. I don't have that story.

Although I was encouraged to do what I wanted, I began to realize I was perceived to be a pretty, charismatic girl. There wasn't much expectation for smarts. In and outside of school, I was expected to be a model or some artistic career that attributed value to appearance. Nothing much was expected of me academically. Although this was a true side of me, my artistic passion and beauty have never defined me. I am a multi-faceted human being. This was hurtful at times, but I learned to lean into that expectation in my favor. I've learned to be smarter and quieter. I've learned that when people see that you're pretty and quiet, people don't expect you to be so smart. So they'll say just about anything in your presence with the idea that you won't catch on. My dad taught me how to play chess when I was very young. He taught me life strategies that I use to this day. He taught me to be as "dumb as a fox."

Chapter 3

A DREAM DEFERRED

In my last semester of completing my Associate's degree, I received an admission letter from my dream school. It was the opportunity of a lifetime to attend The Fashion Institute of Technology, commonly known as F.I.T. in Manhattan. It was November 2009 and I was ecstatic to continue pursuing my Bachelor's Degree there. I remember reading the letter and saying to myself, "This is it"! This was my ticket out of here. I had wanted a fresh start for a long time. I was 22 years old, still living in my parents' house. I'd never gone away to school. I wanted to live on my own and have a fresh start. I was in a relationship that wasn't going anywhere. It was a very toxic relationship and my home life wasn't perfect either. I felt that this was my big chance to live my dreams in the city. I didn't get to pursue this directly after high school, but that was okay. My chance of a lifetime was here now despite my 4-year delay. I was excited to take on this new journey in "the city that never sleeps". I imagined living either in a dorm or off campus, going to work at a local coffee shop or one of the many stores in the city, and taking classes full-time. I was going to make something of myself. I told my boyfriend at the time that I'd be moving and I told my parents the same.

Towards the end of December, I suddenly became violently ill. I had never experienced a menstrual cycle quite like this one before. I had never had this type of violent illness before either. As my cycle ended, I didn't think anything of it. I just kept on going, preparing for my big move. But then in January when I missed my cycle, I decided to take a pregnancy test.

This was the day that changed my life forever. As I sat in my parents' first-floor half-bathroom and took the pregnancy test, I didn't know what to expect, I didn't know what to hope for. I read the results in the quiet house all by myself. It was a plus sign. It was positive. I was pregnant. I felt joy, disappointment, resentment, anger, and a whole bunch of other emotions that I can't put into words. What was I going to do now? Was my dream of going to F.I.T. dead? I was having many thoughts until I finally decided to continue with my plans to attend F.I.T. in January with my baby in my belly.

Since this was my first time at a university, it was tough. I quickly noticed that things were different than at a community college. They took assignments and deadlines very seriously. For a city school, they had a lot of assignments that required fieldwork in the city during the day. This made it very difficult for me because I was working and living full-time in Long Island. One of the classes that required this fieldwork was journalism. The journalism professor was not lenient in any way, shape, or form. I knew that I could not get to the workshop during the day so I turned in the assignment the best way I knew how. The comments she made to me that day were memorable.

At this time it was April and I was showing. It was clear that I was not simply fat because my frame was only a size 4 but I had a protruding belly that had not been there 3 months earlier. As I stood in front of her with my graded assignment and protruding belly, she looked at me and said, "I've never seen an assignment so far off in my history of teaching." She was an older woman, so this was saying a lot. She went on to say, "I showed it to another colleague and they were stunned as well." I gave the excuse that I worked a full-time job during the day, commuting from Long Island, and it was impossible for me to get to the required exhibit.

I struggled commuting and it only became more difficult. It was springtime and I remember this day like it was yesterday. It was a balmy, sunset evening and I was running up the train station stairs. I was trying to catch the train that I heard pulling up to the platform. I was wearing a white peacoat with colorful embroidery and a shiny engagement ring on my left ring finger. My shoulder-length hair was blowing in the wind as I was running up the stairs to catch the train with a laptop case, my purse, and a bag from Dunkin' Donuts that I grabbed on the way to the train. I was hungry, tired, and I had just gotten off a full day at work. I got to the top of the stairs and noticed that the train was still there. There was so much hope in my heart. As I ran full speed towards the train, I got in front of the train doors and felt good about making it. Suddenly, the train doors closed in my face and the train took off. By this point, I was 4 months pregnant. There I was on the platform feeling defeated and devastated. The next train wouldn't arrive for another 45 minutes to an hour and I'd miss my evening class. I didn't know what was going to happen to my grades, but I knew that this wouldn't be good because I had missed instruction time before. Feeling defeated, I turned around and went back down the platform. I made it safely down the platform, got into my car, and went home.

Driving home, I thought to myself, "I'm pregnant, couldn't the train conductor see my belly? Why did he let the doors close?" "Didn't anyone see me running towards the train?" "Why didn't anyone attempt to hold the doors open for me?" I missed another class, but there was nothing I could do about it. I tried my best. I ended up getting a "C" in that class which was the lowest grade I received in all my years at F.I.T.

Chapter 4

A WEDDING, A BABY, AND POSTPARTUM DEPRESSION

I finally completed my spring semester at F.I.T. with an average of 3.0. This was in May 2010. Shortly after that, I commenced planning a wedding. This was a surprisingly sad time for me. I was excited to be getting married, as I had seen in the fairy tale movies, but this wasn't the way I wanted it to go down. I always imagined myself marrying someone I was madly in love with, going to a fancy bridal store, picking out the biggest and most bridal-looking dress that I could set my eyes on, and just dancing off into the sunset to start a family thereafter. Although my life didn't look anything like this, I was still going through with the wedding. This was not the way I thought my life would be but this was what I decided to do.

The next few months were a whirlwind. I moved out of my parents' house, moved in with my fiance, and got hitched. The next step was to have the baby. He was due in September. The time leading up to his birth I'd say was pretty easy. I ate what I wanted, I got special treatment, and I even learned how to make maternity clothes out of regular women's clothing. I rarely shopped in the Maternity section. The only things I bought from Maternity were pants and my church dresses. For the rest, I wore oversized, plus-sized, or extra-large clothes. It worked out fine for me. Once September came, I had my baby. He was beautiful, healthy, and full of life. At least this part was what I imagined. The hospital staff were really helpful and cared for him so I could get some sleep after I gave birth. I learned to breastfeed and all the things that moms learn to do in the hospital. It was really surreal to me. I was really a mother. The days that followed thereafter were a mix of terror, grief, excitement, and other compelling emotions. I'd describe it as one of the worst periods of my life. I hadn't expected what was going to happen next, but it was coming.

Postpartum depression had a grip on me. This was something that no one told me could happen to me. No one told me that it was not unusual for a mom to feel disconnected from her baby. No one forewarned me that I'd feel like I was in a fog just existing and it would be very hard to get out of it. I struggled for my life. Shortly after my son was born he was diagnosed with colic. Colic is a condition where there is gas in the baby's tummy that is very uncomfortable and downright painful to the baby. This makes them cry a lot. And cry he did. At the time, there weren't any formulas for colic. I took care of him day and night for the first 6 weeks. I cared for him crying, and screaming, all while dealing with my own postpartum lack of mobility. I was also still going through the postpartum changes of bleeding and having to care for my own health at the same time. Up to this point, I had never changed a diaper in my life. My son's father went to work during the daytime, attended church services in the evening, and often found things to do even on his days off, which left me with the baby most of the time. Some days the baby would cry, and I'd cry more. It was a cry fest. Some days when the baby would start crying, I'd start crying too and the baby would stop. I felt so frustrated with the crying and not knowing what to do. I didn't know how I could continue living like this. I wasn't getting much help or support and I felt alone. One evening, I was in real tears. Not the fake ones that we pretend like we're doing to get the baby to stop crying, but real tears from my soul. My life was in shambles. I didn't know what to do and I didn't know who to call without feeling like I was burdening them. Some days, I didn't even want to live. I thought about a song that I'd sing when I looked into his little eyes. With tears streaming down my face, I'd begin to sing:

I'm not a perfect person.
There are many things I wish I didn't do.
But I continue learning,
I never meant to do those things to you.
And so, I have to say before I go...

That I just want you to know...
I've found a reason for me,
To change who I used to be,
A reason to start over new...
And the reason is you

I'm sorry that I hurt you.
It's something I must live with every day.
And all the pain I put you through,
I wish that I could take it all away.
And be the one who catches all your tears.
That's why I need you to hear...

I've found a reason for me...
To change who I used to be,
A reason to start over new...

And the reason is you
And the reason is you
And the reason is you
And the reason is you!

This is a song called "*The Reason*" by the band Hoobastank. It described exactly how I felt. When I felt that I couldn't protect him from getting colic, I wasn't good at applying his diaper, and I didn't feel as connected to him as I felt that I should've been. I sang and I cried. I cried and I sang. I didn't know what else to do. I didn't have anyone I felt I could trust with the information that I was struggling with. I wasn't okay. Anytime anyone asked me how I was doing, I'd say "fine". In hindsight, they could tell I wasn't fine. I didn't have the words to express how I was feeling without breaking down and crying in public. Were they asking because they really cared? Were they asking because they were looking for gossip? Were they asking because they actually wanted to roll up their sleeves and be there for me? Those three questions, I couldn't determine from that simple question, "How are you?" A lot of people ask that question, but they don't show up when you need them. I didn't have a lot of friends at that time. The ones I did have, I considered "surface-level friends" as it's called. We never got into personal details with each other, we just had lunch together every now and then. I didn't have anyone that I felt would help me out confidentially. I continued to sing "*The Reason*" to my baby when I felt moved, never with a dry eye. I also sang "*For Once In My Life*" by Stevie Wonder which would make me feel better about this gift that God had given me. For years I had dreamed about being a mother to a beautiful, healthy child.

For once in my life, I have someone who needs me
Someone I've needed so long
For once, unafraid, I can go where life leads me
Somehow I know I'll be strong
For once I can touch what my heart used to dream of
Long before I knew
Someone warm like you
Would make my dreams come true
For once in my life, I won't let sorrow hurt me
Not like it's hurt me before
For once, I have something I know won't desert me
I'm not alone anymore
For once I can say, "This is mine, you can't take it"
As long as I know I have love, I can make it
For once in my life, I have someone who needs me.

This song made me feel better and it also kept my baby entertained. He seemed to like these songs. He stopped crying when I'd sing. But sometimes, I didn't feel like singing. I just felt like crying, curling up in a ball, and wishing the world would go away.

My husband at this time wasn't understanding at all. He still expected me to cook, clean, and do all the things that wives are "supposed to do". I'd never been demeaned this way in my life. I felt as though I wasn't even human. I was expected to function as a machine. I couldn't meet those expectations at all. I felt subhuman and that I didn't deserve to live. I couldn't do anything right and was berated every day because of it. I desperately wanted to go back to work to escape the nightmare I was living.

Chapter 5
WORK TO THE RESCUE! ... OR MAYBE NOT

When I finally returned to work, I was reminded of how much I hated my job. I hated working in a call center, from the depths of my soul. I hated the fact that my life had been reduced to working in insurance. There were no high-paying fashion jobs in the suburbs outside of working at the mall. My mornings included getting up early, getting my son ready, and taking him to daycare before work. I was late to work every day for my 9 a.m. start time. Ten to fifteen minutes late, every day. My start time would get pushed back a few minutes in the name of "flextime", but I'd still be late. I just couldn't get it together. After about a month, my supervisor put me on a warning - "Be on time or you're going to lose your job." I tried, but I'd still be sporadically late after that.

Finally, a position opened up with later hours in a different department. It was for a job that I actually found interesting in the Investigations

Department. I applied for it expeditiously. Within a few weeks, I heard back that I didn't get that position, but they found one that would better suit me in the same department. I had secured a job I didn't even apply for. Won't He do it? It truly was a dream job, to say the least. I hated working in a call center, but this job made it easier to go to work every day. It was less phone calls and more of actually handling cases.

I could use the investigative skills that I've always had. My first major in college was Investigative Journalism. I was editor of my high school newspaper for years and I was a pretty good writer. My role model was Barbara Walters. I loved watching her interviews. She had a way of being captivating and endearing while getting to the meat of the conversation with whomever she interviewed. I interned at a local newspaper during my last semester of high school into the summer. As an intern, my job was to write up the press releases I was given. I was expected to ask very few questions. Well, I could ask questions but then I'd risk no longer getting press releases and being relegated to some other, less fun task. With the normal expectations, if there wasn't any big news that the head writers hadn't already picked up, press release write-ups were my main job. I once wrote a front-page article for the newspaper. When I saw it on the newsstands on my campus, I began beaming with pride. I made it! I was big time now. That was a very proud moment for me.

I also remember going to the local train station and interviewing passengers about the new changes in service. My fellow interns and I went back to the office and we wrote the stories together. It was a highlight to be "in the field" doing the work. I needed this freedom to write and to be creative, on a regular basis. I needed to be able to do a proper investigation of important issues in every story. However, a preference for captivating stories wasn't available to interns. I changed my major to Marketing within my first semester. I went on to graduate with my Associate's Degree in Marketing in December 2009.

So here I was, working in the Investigation Department in January 2011, 3 months after giving birth to my first child. The work did give me time to do proper investigations, I had the proper tools to do the investigations, and I worked with tenured associates who guided me along the way. When I was fully set up in this job 9 months in, I decided to go back to school.

In Fall 2011, I went back to F.I.T. to finish what I had started. I had a once-a-week, in-person class that would require me to wake up at 4 AM, catch a train by 6 AM, and be at class by 8 AM. I'm not a morning person, so this was torture. I had to gather a sleeping newborn, get him over to childcare, and make sure I had everything I needed before dawn. I missed the train occasionally, but most of the time I caught it. I discovered - it feels good to start your day before sunrise. By the time everyone was just getting up, my day was well underway. After my class ended at 11 AM, I headed back home to start my job from 1- 9 PM; those days were exhausting. I just wanted to go home and sleep. It was very hard. Some days I'd get home and there would be no food. In hindsight, this was crazy. For the next two semesters, I'd spend days and nights arguing with my husband about going to school to complete my Bachelor's Degree. At the time I had gotten pregnant with my first son, I was in my first semester at F.I.T. pursuing my Bachelor's Degree. There was no way that I'd give that up for any man. My grandmothers taught me better, my mother taught me better, and my aunts taught me better. They impressed upon me: never sacrifice your education for any reason, especially not for a man. After all, my family came to this country for a better life, and as a 1st generation American, I stand on these values. In my second semester, I was signed up for three classes. I was hopeful that after my fall semester, I'd be more experienced to take on an extra class. I couldn't have been more wrong but for unexpected reasons.

I was being berated day and night for all the things that I couldn't do. My husband, at the time, would tell me things like "You don't need to go to school" and "You need to focus on being a mother and a wife." I'd argue back, "What does that even mean?!" There is no other focus, my goal for getting my Bachelor's Degree was to provide a better life for myself and my family. I was home most of the time. I planned carefully to elongate my school days so that everything fit. My husband did not have any degrees or special skills to speak of and his job options were very limited. I was frustrated, exhausted, overwhelmed, and I still was trying to make a connection with my baby. I needed to get my Bachelor's Degree.

Chapter 6

THE UNSTOPPABLE WOMAN

As a woman with a child now, I wanted nothing to do with limited job options. If I lost my job and could not get another in insurance, I'd at least have a Bachelor's Degree to fall back on. I never told him this in these terms, because I knew that he already insinuated that I was going to use my education as a tool to no longer need him for financial support. With my Bachelor's Degree, the world was my oyster. It didn't matter what I got my degree in. Although I did love marketing, the standard for having a Bachelor's Degree in the field of business was something that got me into doors that not having one wouldn't. My goal was to get my Bachelor's Degree before my son was 5 years old. After all, I only had two years of school left. I think an extra three years was plenty of cushion room just in case I failed a class or had any other changes that would result in a different plan. My plan was solid. After my first year back at F.I.T., the pressure at work began mounting. My work environment turned out to be very toxic. I was berated with personal questions and inappropriate conversations on a regular basis, even when I said I was not comfortable. The environment in this particular department had been rumored to be toxic before I got there. I didn't know this but honestly, if I had, I don't think I would've cared. I did my work, I minded my business, and I went home. That has been my motto since I entered the workforce and it has never let me down. So that's what I did. I did my work, I asked questions when I needed to, and then I went home. Between the toxic work environment and the toxic home environment, my mental health began deteriorating. I was reaching my limit. I needed to make some changes.

For one, I needed to get a divorce. There's no way in the hell that I'd let any man stop me from getting my education. I was going to pack up my stuff, my baby, and head back to my mother's house. She would surely understand. This issue wasn't an issue in the house that I grew up in. Getting a good education was one of the reasons we were here in the United States. My values dictated I would be successful in America, starting with a college education. There were no "ifs" "ands" or "buts" about it.

In an attempt to cut my losses, I sent an email to my college professor of the third class I was taking saying I had to withdraw from this class. The berating that I was getting at home was at an all-time high and I felt like I was losing my mind. I did not tell my college professor this. When he asked me why I was withdrawing I simply said, personal issues. He understood and kindly approved my withdrawal.

In the Spring of 2012, I started to consider divorce proceedings. I began separating my stuff, taking care of only me and my son, and I didn't care if we all still lived under the same roof. My soon-to-be ex-husband saw this, and he saw the commotion I was making with my family and at the church that we both attended. He didn't like the commotion and how he was being "exposed", then suddenly his behavior shifted. He began being more supportive of me pursuing my Bachelor's Degree and finalizing this portion of my education. The following Fall semester through my graduation in Spring 2015, he was a lot more supportive than he'd ever been. I had to do a lot of work and I'd sound the alarms when I wasn't getting the support that I needed. I got it done.

There were a few occasions when I could not find childcare and I took my son to class with me. He would sit with his iPad and his headphones next to me in class; this was when he was about 4 years old. I remember one day when I had to take him to my Information Systems class in the computer lab. We were late to class, but that wasn't new. I stumbled into an already commenced class, with my baggage and child, and sat towards the back. The class was amazed at how well my son behaved. Some of them hadn't realized he was there until class was well underway. There was a point where I was not able to see the board over the computers, so I sat in the back of the classroom at an open desk. The professor asked a question that seemed rhetorical, nevertheless, the professor was looking for an answer. He peered over the computers looking for someone to answer his question.

Suddenly, a little hand popped up from the sea of computers. It was my son. The professor called on him, then my son then proceeded to correctly answer the question. The professor was amazed. "Whose child is this?" He questioned. "He's my son," I answered. At that moment, the professor said to the whole class, "You see this young man, everyone?

This young man is the future. He's going to lead all of us. He's going to be something special." The professor continued with the lesson and I couldn't have felt more proud. My son was very smart and he loved school, even from a young age. I attribute some of his love for school to coming with me. I have a picture of him with his little book bag standing in front of the campus directory looking so confused. Little did he know, adults would genuinely be confused by that map too.

In May 2015, I was honored to have my then 4-year-old son see me walk across the stage and graduate with my Bachelor's Degree. This was one of the proudest moments of my life. My son may not have been aware of everything that was going on, but he'll have this memory forever.

Chapter 7

BUILDING BACK MOMENTUM

Within the same year, I got my Bachelor's Degree, bought my first property, and got pregnant with my second son. Things were looking up. Most of all, I was overwhelmed by the high of getting my Bachelor's Degree. I was always made to feel that I wasn't smart and that I wasn't good enough since I was a child. My sister was considered the smart one and nothing much was really expected of me. I was told regularly, "It's okay if you don't go to college, you can go to trade school." While trade school wasn't a bad option, it wasn't my goal. I wanted to graduate from college. I was really overwhelmed by the fact that I had achieved what once felt like it was only a dream. I thought to myself, what else could I do that would surpass my expectations of myself? So, I bought a house on Beyoncé's birthday in 2015. Things were looking up for me. Beyoncé songs were playing on the radio all day and all night. I was overjoyed.

A few months later I got pregnant with my second son. This pregnancy, and thereafter, would go better than the first. My relationship with my husband was better than ever at this time. My oldest son was also such a big help to me. He helped in getting the little one's bottles and clothes; he was great at being Mommy's little helper. I felt solidified as an adult now. When I had my first son at 23, I still felt like a child trying to figure things out. By now, at the age of 29, I was a woman who was a wife and a mother of two children. I took those responsibilities very seriously. Even when I was 9 months pregnant with my second child, I'd still go to the park with my oldest. I had to entertain him, it wasn't his fault I was pregnant. By the time the baby was born, I'd strap the little one up in his stroller and we'd all go to the park.

I was very involved in my son's schooling. I joined the PTA when my son started Pre-K and even found time to volunteer on several committees at work. I got promoted again and was a rising star at work, superstar wife, and superstar mother. I was doing it all. From cooking multiple times a week to taking care of the house, and everything else. I was the perfect mother and wife in my mind. I was living the good life for the first few months after having the baby, after that, things got rocky. I had tried to do everything in my power to get to the next level at work, but because of my child care or lack thereof, I was not able to progress very far. This was extremely frustrating for me. I'd see "young kids", fresh out of college, with no work experience, getting promoted ahead of me. This pissed me off, for lack of a better term. I felt discriminated against and there was nothing I could do about it. I had to leave on time to get my son from the babysitter. I couldn't stay late and work longer or harder like the single people could. It was infuriating and defeating at times to see others with less knowledge and experience getting jobs I deserved.

The daily workload was very heavy. I could get it done because I was skillful, I just didn't have enough time in the day. I attempted to pump and store my breast milk at work, but within a few weeks, I realized that being away from my desk caused me to fall behind. I had to give up breastfeeding for this reason. I resented the job for that reason, amongst others. This employer had passively instituted a very discriminatory practice. I tried to apply for positions in different departments and to other companies, but I had no success for the next year.

The next year, when I turned thirty, was one of the hardest years of my life. What saved this year for me, was my trip to Paris, France on my 30th birthday. Paris, France is said to be one of the fashion capitals of the world. I've dreamed of going to this place since I was a child. In all my dreams, this was another dream come true for me. I was so happy to be there. I bought clothes there that I still get compliments on to this day. After my birthday trip, I began to feel depressed and defeated again. I walked around very pessimistically for over a year.

One day, I told my sister of my work woes and she asked to see my resume. Reluctantly, I gave it to her. I thought to myself, why can't people see my experience on this paper and just take it for what it is? To my surprise, she fixed up my resume and I had a job offer within the next few months. I couldn't understand how something so simple could be holding me back from so many different opportunities. My experience was the same, I was the same person, but with just a few changes to my resume, a huge change occurred in my world. After months of salary negotiation, I started a new position at a better company. It was a dream job for me. Here, there were no overtime requirements. I could just do my job and go home. There were opportunities to work from home, the office space was comfortable, they offered free refreshments, and it was very modernly decorated. I started to think, what else could go right?

I found this comfortable job that gave me the freedom to do what I wanted, so what now? I started to do what I always do when I'm bored - get a Professional Certification. When I finished the professional certification, I thought, what else? I've always been into fashion, but I've never gotten to finish my studies at F.I.T. I certainly didn't have the time or physical freedom to go back now. I thought of how else I could start a career as a Fashion Stylist.

There was a new position for a Stylist at Macy's. I'd do both jobs at the same time! Now that I didn't have school to go to part-time or full-time, I had some free time on my hands. So I took a part-time job at Macy's for a couple of hours a week, just to learn the business of what a Stylist does. To my surprise, there was no "Stylist" position. They had me listed as a "Fitting Room Associate". I cringed so hard when I found that out. I'm nobody's "Fitting Room Associate". Within a month I quit. Then, the next best thing happened. There was a fairly new app called Instagram, which I heard that you could get money from posting pictures of your outfits. This was in 2019 and Instagram was more popular than Facebook, with Millenials.

Chapter 8

PLAN B FOR THE WIN!

At this point, I fell back on plan B, which was Instagram. When I started to live for myself and do the things that made me happy, I started to notice a very clear deterioration in what I thought was a marriage. There was never an "us" in my happiness. He felt my happiness needed to revolve around making him happy. Now, at the age of 32, I was a fully grown woman, no longer easy to manipulate with psychological warfare. I had enough! This was finally the end. I was better off alone. What I came to realize: I was married to myself. There was no actual commitment from both sides. When I became blatantly aware of this, I was devastated. This was the only boyfriend I'd had since I was 18. Here I was, now 32, getting a divorce from the same man, after over a decade. What was I supposed to do at this point? How could I start over when my entire world, my entire adult identity was tied into being with this man?

I seriously felt that I was losing my natural mind. I began going to therapy to cope with some of the changes that I was going through mentally and emotionally. Therapy helped a lot. There were many times when I didn't know which way was up. I had been private my whole entire life until this point. I've never told my friends exactly what I was going through at home or any of my personal business. So when I finally opened up to my friends and my family about what I was going through, they were shocked. I received an outpouring of love and support from people who truly, genuinely cared about me. I wish I had spoken up sooner. I wish I hadn't just suffered in the dark, feeling alone.

In the months following, friends and family would offer to take me out so I'd feel better. The issue was, when I looked in my closet, I had nothing to wear. That's when it hit me. For the last 10 years of my life following high school, I didn't go anywhere. I just went to church, work, work events, PTA meetings, school functions, and home. I didn't really go anywhere that required me

to dress up or have fun. I had been in school just about the whole time. I had started college in 2005 and I was on my pursuit of a Bachelor's Degree for the next 10 years, through hell or high water. I reflected on my life which mainly consisted of going to school full-time, working full-time, going on class trips with my son, attending daytime school events, and volunteering at work. With all of that, I still managed to get home before nightfall to be with my family.

I'd spent my life up to this point doing all the things other people expected, wanted, and needed me to do. But what about me? I asked myself this when I found myself crying to myself on the floor. I couldn't understand how this was happening, I had done everything that I was supposed to do, yet I ended up here. I asked God why He would let this happen to me. His response was that I had a choice. I didn't like that. I wanted to have a different option, not here. I spent my days and nights agonizing over all the mistakes I had made and all the ways I could have avoided going down this path. I beat myself up over all the things I should have never tolerated. I thought about all of the times that I was just a "fool for love". I'll never make that mistake again. I'll join a convent before I ever get married again.

I was now a divorced, single mother, left with an ubiquitous feeling of shame. Yes, I did get married very young, but was I crazy enough to think that this would be one of those 1940s things that would last forever? Maybe I was too naive to think about the circumstances of women in marriage in the 1940s. Most women didn't have jobs. Most depended on their husbands for money and for freedom. Most tolerated things they shouldn't have in the name of financial and economic stability. I'm a new-age woman. I need not tolerate any of that. I was considered the "breadwinner" and by all accounts, I'm way better off by myself. So I had to learn to discover who that person was at 32 years old after being married for almost a decade. I had to try to find who that little girl was inside of me who was now a mature adult. Therapy helped me a lot with that. I attribute my stability to prayer, faith, and just good old therapy. I've learned to develop values over the years that have been evolving to this point.

Chapter 9

REDESIGNING ME

I learned a lot about myself by going out and mingling with other people. I learned who I clicked with, and who I didn't click with. I've learned what scenes I will and won't tolerate. I spent time going to events that I thought were fun and cool. I realized that when I initially got dressed to go out at the beginning of my divorce, I was stuck in a period of time. I wanted to be 18 again, but I wasn't. I wanted to wear the stuff that I saw the young people wearing. However, with a baby belly, and different dimensions in my body, I could not wear those things anymore. I had to rediscover my style all over again. I had to discover my identity... all by myself. I hadn't had the opportunity as many young girls do to discover their identity in college and the years following. I was tied up very young and my identity was yet to be written. I'd try different outfit combinations and eventually, I landed on things that fit my body properly, were age-appropriate, and made me feel sexy. Because after all, I was still only in my 30s. I was not a 70 or 80-year-old grandma. I needed to dress, look, and feel my age. I was very restricted with my time battling divorce proceedings and caring for my children. I didn't have a lot of time to take on another Styling job. So I found myself on the internet becoming a budding content creator. Then COVID-19 hit and the world shut down.

Surviving the year 2020, COVID-19, and the global shutdown, was a lesson for us all. I became a school teacher and gym teacher, I learned to do my work and homework with the kids simultaneously, and I learned so many other skills I didn't know that I was capable of. It was a hard time for me, like for most people. I was adjusting to my new life while adjusting to a world that seemed unreal outside. The kids were doing their best and I was doing my best to support them. I appreciated teachers this year more than I ever had in my life. Luckily for me, our school district opened in Fall 2020, so I got a little breather. However, I maintained the same habits from the pandemic: I'd wake up early in the morning and be in bed by 2 AM just about every day. These were habits I developed to get my kids logged on to school and then do my work later in the day, once I put them to bed. I worked around the clock. When they went back to school, I needed to retrain myself to regular business hours. Instead, I filled those hours with making content. I worked my "9 to 5", then I worked from "5 to 9" on content, and sometimes I worked until 2 AM. I did whatever I had to do to get my content out there, get my work done, and still find time to enjoy my life.

It took a lot of time to curate looks that I felt would resonate with my audience. From my marketing degrees, I knew I couldn't sell anything without an audience. That much made sense from social media. I learned to connect with other creatives and business owners with a like-minded agenda to collaborate on projects that suited our collective needs. I began attending events, networking meetings, online seminars, master classes, courses, workbooks, you name it, I did it. I was doing everything I could to learn about business in a way that I hadn't learned from getting a business degree. My marketing classes didn't teach me how to use social media. I was figuring this out all on my own. Building an audience seemed like something that was so far away. When I got to Instagram, there were people with thousands and millions of followers. How was I supposed to catch up with that?

Slowly, but surely, I successfully began to grow my following. I met some helpful and kind-hearted individuals who poured into me and pointed me in the right direction. For most of 2020, I focused heavily on content creation. By the end of the year, I was booking styling clients. I'd document all of the work that I did, post it on social media, and continue to get business based on my work. It was like an app for me to get and share work. It was great. In 2021, I got the courage to move on from my insurance job. I found myself in a position that would teach more about the fashion industry and about the clients that I aspired to reach. I learned so much about the business, fashion psychology, brands, trends, and my target market. By being exposed to things that I hadn't been exposed to before, I also was able to refine my own personal style.

In conclusion, my journey as detailed in this book has been a profound and transformative one. I've learned and grown immensely up to this point, and I'm eternally grateful for everyone who has and continues to support me. As I look forward to what's next, my heart is filled with excitement. My story is a testament to the power of personal growth, resilience, and self-discovery, and I hope it inspires others to embark on their unique paths with the same courage and unapologetic authenticity that I've found.

CONNECT WITH BRENDA

Brenda Gonzalez
Owner/Lead Stylist
Styled By B

- www.styledbyb.net
- @imstyledbyb
- info@styledbyb.net